How to *Get & Keep*

a **KING**

The Biblical Way

by Olive Swan

© 2019 Olive Swan
Printed in the U.S.A.
First Printing 2017

All rights reserved. No part of this publication may be reproduced, distributed, or transmitted in any form or by any means including photocopying, recording, or other electronic / mechanical methods, without the prior written permission of the publisher, except in the case of brief quotations, along with a citing of the source, in non-commercial uses permitted by copyright law.

For permission requests, email the author with the subject line "Attention: book permission request" at thefeminineprincess@gmail.com

Dedication

For all the women, whose love is as a betta fish in her heart, seeking one, whose own betta fish causes hers to flutter and twirl...

The Secret of the Lord is with them that fear Him and He will show them His covenant ~ Psalm 25:14

Contents:

Entryway

Rebekah

Ruth

Esther

Abigail

Fresh Thought

Building Your Case

Keeping 7 Keys for Life

Reflections

Spiritual Insurance

About the Author

Contact

Entryway

Because Jesus' Kingdom is not of this earth, He is exotic, since we call someone or something that is far, fascinating, and foreign, *exotic*. Because I am of His Kingdom, I too am exotic. And I have exotic thoughts, exotic ways, exotic movements, exotic scents, exotic music...exotic *everything*.

Come delicate petals, and enter this exotic world with me, where we will learn an exotic way, to getting and keeping a godly man. Explore each one of the songs our exquisite maidens of the Word of God have sung for us. Let's listen to their melodies and compose our own song.

But before you step through this ancient path I want to remind you:

"For even Christ pleased not Himself"
~Roman 15:3

The world's counsel today would tell any becoming woman to position herself so that the man pleases her, before she can accept him. They meticulously expound on how she should make herself outwardly beautiful, learn to manipulate the psychology of a man, and then start to control him emotionally and behaviorally through her actions, speech, and personality. After playing tete a tete with him by appearances and seeming absences of such, she receives a man that desires nothing more in life than to have her, adore her, please her, and serve her.

Dear lovelies, this is worship! Worship belongs to One only, and that is our Lord Jesus!! We are only supposed to worship Him. To worship a human is a perversion of His way. The Biblical examples the Holy Spirit showed us, has a different perspective for a woman to be selected by a man, dear pumpkin. It is a spirit of humility. This is the only godly and righteous way to connect with your future husband. You are not to seek to please yourself, if you desire to imitate Jesus, because humility is the only way to receive honor in the Kingdom of God. When you understand that and decide to follow the model of Christ, you will receive the benefits you have been so deeply desiring.

As I go into depth about this God-prescribed way dear buttercup of the Lord, you must keep in mind that you are not to follow this pattern with EVERY man you are approached by. You are to use your God-given discernment on who to share your precious blessings with. Ask the Holy Spirit to lead you.

This may be difficult to determine if you have experienced patterns of unworthy men. If this is so, you must begin to change yourself as well as sort out the qualified from the unqualified. If you need help getting started, here are 3 steps to move into position:

1. Pray: Dear Heavenly Father, I bless you as the One who Creates the

Heavens and the Earth. You said man may build, but you are the author of all things. We believe and know you have made everything we see, everything we have, and everything we yet crave. We ask you to give us not only discernment to show us who is worthy of being with us, but also show us what to do, where to go, and how to act, in order to be qualified to receive what we are seeking You for. We trust your process and promise to do what you ask, in Jesus Name, Amen.

2. Start surrounding yourself with people of a higher level of thinking and acting, that you want to be with. Become friends with both women

and men of a higher caliber than you and learn everything you can from them. Learn how they move, what they say, what they read, what they watch, how they think, etc..

The fact that you are reading this book, my truffle pop, is the evidence that you have not yet entered the realm of where you need to be with the right man for you. The Holy Spirit will do a wondrous work on you that will change this truth, if you allow and accept it. Then you will be able to find the man you want and the one that God wants you to have. This process will occur at the speed of your willingness and condition of your heart, mind, and spirit.

3. Start shedding, cutting, and discarding everything related to the past. Your past self, your past season, your past thoughts, your past ways, your past relics. Everything...Out! Out of your house, out of your realm, out of your life. It has got to *go,* in order for you to be worthy to enter into this new dimension where your dream knight dwells.

Are you Ready, dear precious one? Open your Bibles with me, as we study the songs of the fair damsels in the Word of God...

Rebekah

~Genesis 24:9-67

Composition:

* A Natural beauty and virgin

* In the process of working her daily tasks
* Willing to be interrupted and inconvenienced to assist another
* Quickly helped someone in need
* Offering to go beyond what she was asked
* Good attitude during hard labor
* Answering any inquiries truthfully
* Immediately accepting and acclimating to her new journey, role, and life

<u>Verse</u>:

Your attraction is not in the

adornment of jewels, makeup, and materials of clothing, but from an inner beauty that glows on the outside, giving you a natural loveliness. This inner beauty must not be polluted from the touch of men, but kept pure from yearning of lust disguised as love. Purify your body, minds, and hearts before the Lord

Chorus:

When I am asked for help, and if it's safe and possible, I will help the person and go beyond in offering my kind assistance

Bridge:

Have a quickness in your spirit to complete tasks for others

Decrescendo:

Follow your intuition as you finish any instructions given, then be open to receive good consequences

Arrangement:

Keep a joyous sweet attitude throughout the process while staying flexible and adaptable to change

Song Theme:

"I am here for you..."

Ruth

~Ruth 3:1-18, 4:1-13

Composition:

* Build and have good character

* Work for what you currently need instead of expecting a hand out
* Put yourself in position to be seen of good men
* Seek favor from God and man
* Wash yourself
* Anoint yourself
* Clothe yourself
* Humble yourself
* Wait for a response

<u>Verse</u>:

You will work on yourself wholly, internally and externally, to prepare for a man

Chorus:

I am aligned in harmony with the timing the presenting of myself for a relationship and it occurs only after I have brought myself to a high level of excellence mentally, spiritually, and physically

Bridge:

Put yourself in visible or public position to be examined

Decrescendo:

Wait patiently to see how he will respond to you, without impatience, forcing, helping, nor reminding him

Arrangement:

Have such outstanding character, that even strangers, friends, and family alike take notice

Song Theme:

"I have perfected myself for you..."

Esther

~Esther 2:7-18

<u>Composition:</u>

* Natural beauty

* Obedience to those in authority over you

* Please the associates, workers, and friends of your intended

* Receive what is given to you happily

* Prepare for one year to meet your king (with myrrh, sweet odors, and other ways purifying yourself)

* Cast out a spirit of greed and pride

* Follow instructions given

* Obtain grace and favor in the sight the King

Verse:

You will obey any authority God

places over you until He transfers you to a new realm when you excel in what you are required to do

Chorus:

I will purify myself with the oils of the holy anointing and the perfumes of loveliness by first being healed of any internal and external dis-ease and then perfecting the beauty I was given, inside and out

Bridge:

Seek favor from those in your immediate environment

Decrescendo:

Present yourself in the best light at all times, as people with varying social statuses are watching you and will speak of your spirit

Arrangement:

Strict adherence to protocol and any suggestions in an unknown environment, are necessary for a success

Song Theme:

"I am approved of by all..."

Abigail

~I Samuel 25:14-42

Composition:

* Listen to the whole situation before reacting

* Prepare his request quickly and don't waste time talking to everyone about it

* Get appropriate help if necessary

* Meet and deliver it to him personally

* Humble self before him

* Be willing to accept any blame even if it's not your fault

* Speak kind words to him

* Recognize his greatness by acknowledging his victorious past and tie that into his glorious future

* Ask him to remember you

* Keep quiet and wait for his response

* When he sends for you, immediately respond favorably

<u>Verse:</u>

You will please him by giving him his heart's desires, his likes or preferences, and his needs for the hour

Chorus:

I will have a humble spirit in all I do, but especially when it comes to my love

Bridge:

Recognize who he really is then show him respect and honor because of it

Decrescendo:

Request his remembrance of you, as you show him kindness

Arrangement:

Deliver his wants with haste and gentleness

Song Theme:

"I will serve you what you want..."

Fresh Thought

My magnetic Princess, settle this today in your hearts:

Dating, boyfriend / girlfriend, live in lover, friends with benefits, etc.. all are concepts that are foreign and profane to the ones who truly belong to the Lord. God has warned us not to take the ways of other nations as we live among them, for they would surely turn our hearts from Him and His ways, to bring about a curse upon us. For further study read Jeremiah 10:2-3 and Deuteronomy 18:9-14.

Decide now, that you want to live

your life *Biblically in every way* without compromise. Unless you do not believe the Word of God is the highest and supreme form of truth given to us by His Holy Spirit, please follow after the true ancient ways that still yield pure fruit. Any argument that one can present in favor of the current culture stems from rebellion, doubt, and fear, as well as leaning to his own understanding.

If you trust in the Lord all your heart, which I believe you do dear radiant heart, then you don't have nor put confidence in your own analysis of a mate. Your resources, knowledge, and mentality are limited, evolving, and myopic. The Lord's knows all things in all dimensions at all times.

Here are two strong possible illustrations, but not absolute models, to support that using your own judgment only could lead to future demise, delay, or disappointment:

Scenario one: A man has checked all the boxes and she is the one. She is perfect for him in support, vision, and personality. They get married, but God brings about some type of change into the man's life. This woman, whom he picked for the current season in his life, is ill-suited for the new season God is bringing him into. He starts to feel uneasy about their relationship and soon seeks a divorce. She can't flow with his new life and she wonders what happened to the (old) man she married.

Scenario two:
Everyone keeps telling this man that a certain woman is perfect for him. Yet he just doesn't see it. It's not that she isn't attractive nor sweet, but she has some personality traits that might challenge him. She also is focusing on slightly different goals than he is. Plus, he always wanted a woman with a certain physical or psychological characteristic and she doesn't have it. He passes on her.

Several years later, he meets her again but this time she is married. After a brief but cordial meet, he realizes, that she was the one God wanted him with for his personal growth, maturity, and support for his life. It's too late, as she has moved on. He is now seeking God to send him another one like her.

Caution yourselves lovely tulips, that you do not fall into these traps.

Building Your Case

Dear delicate one, there are some logical defenses might be presented against your new faith and understanding. Let's take a look at the chief ones:

The main argument I repetitively hear is: *"What if you get married, not having tested the sexual aspect of the relationship only to be disappointed? Now you are stuck with that person for life...!"*

Oh lollipops, there is so much to address here! First, this statement is mostly made male unbelievers. Or I least that's whom I've heard make that statement. No, I don't mean atheists nor agnostics, I mean people that don't know nor rely on the veracity of God's character and promises. Unbelievers.

Next, it shows how base their thoughts are, as they are reducing a long-term committed relationship to their finite evaluation on how good the 'sex' was with the person at one particular time. *(Let me insert here -no pun intended- that I believe sex is very important in the continued connection of a committed couple and I honor it as a wonderful, yet sacred act only to be shared with a married hetero couple, as patterned by the Bible.)*

If we are loving one another as Christ loves us, sex is not primary in *evaluating* our mate's qualification for a marriage. In addition, little alluring blossom, this intimate experience will be worked out for the best of both parties (all God-made couples have testified to this truth).

Sex is also not really about receiving all the pleasure, but giving it. Once you release the demand to be pleased and instead focus on pleasing your partner, you will receive the greatest pleasure you so desire too.

Marriage is about the adjustment and growth of two individuals, with sex included. So it may or may not be perfect during the first time or few times, but that's not the whole purpose right? Isn't it the fact that you are now living with the love of your soul's life??

That alone satisfies me regardless how a man 'performs' for me. One should be sensitive to the other too, for he or she may be shy, nervous, embarrassed, insecure, etc.. If your mate can't consider your feelings, relax your spirit, and comfort your concerns, then whose job it is to do those things, doll-face?

Lastly, that statement reflects the ultimate distrust in God, whom created every distinct thing about you, knows what you like and don't like, and what you need in every hour. If you've been faithful to Him, He will give you the desire of your heart if you trust in Him to do so. You cannot convince me that after full confidence in and obedience to Him, that He would give a person someone that greatly displeases him or her. Just look at the Scriptures, which are full of illustrations of those who received the promises of God, after waiting patiently in faith, according to Hebrews chapter 6.

I have also witnessed two different

experiences where God brought something in a person's mate that they didn't like nor want, but <u>it was always in direct correlation to something the Lord was purifying in them</u>. Don't think that the Lord, whom is very much involved in His people's lives, won't bring the very thing a person doesn't desire at that time, only to mature the person or to bring about His purpose. It is still ultimately His way and His will, and as believers, we yield to this. (See the story of Samson's first wife or David's first betrothed, Saul's daughter, or Hosea's wife, as perfect examples of God working his purpose through a person's mate that seemed an unlikely match.)

The other argument I hear often, o striking one, is: *"but how can you make a decision if you don't get to know someone first?"*

Getting to know someone, dear plum drop, is man's way qualifying a person. God's way is different from our way, especially in the assessment of a person, and we see that clearly and repetitively shown Scripture. The Lord always announces to the one whom perceives, that "This is the one whom I have chosen". God qualifies a person by seeing their heart and preparing them for their destiny. Man tends to look on the outside appearance and also can only judge from a limited perspective, while God says, "I know the end from the beginning" and "I have good thoughts towards your future". Who wouldn't want our all-knowing God to pick our mate for us?

The only cultural positions accepted by the Lord are: single, betrothed, or married, dear honey crepe. Those are the only examples of relationship statuses we have in the Word of God, which we are supposed to follow with a whole heart.

When we delve into the principles behind a couple being brought together by the Lord in Scriptures, I find three:

1. A man and woman were hand-picked for one another by the Lord
2. A couple were chosen to build a future and a promise that the Lord had given
3. They were positioned to grow a family while staying together in love for life. Divorces, among couples God chose and connected, did not exist

In addition, my peach nectar, I do not believe in long engagements when you are CERTAIN the relationship is of the Lord. Especially when the couple is of equal mind in values, has approximately the same spiritual maturity, and shares similar life goals. Of course, if there are doubts based on facts, experiences, or intuition, little hot-fudge, then please examine all of them, for they could be the Holy Ghost speaking to you and warning you.

Long engagements also tend to give opportunity to three unfortunate things:
1. Human perception and judgment overshadowing the promise of a wedding
2. The use the time by the enemy to cause a dissention to rise
3. Excuses for more delay and doubt to enter while sin lies at the door

In looking at our current traditions and culture, I've found a pattern that many relationship coaches and expert authors give women today. Here are their main rules:

1. Don't accept last minute dates
2. Be busy with your own life
3. See other men simultaneously
4. Wait for him to make the first move
5. Train him to work with your schedule

Yet, in every Biblical example shared in this book, carrot cake, we've witnessed four women who married great warriors of God, that broke every last one of these 'dating' rules. And all of their marriages lasted till one....of....them....died.

In understanding and agreeing to all these things, we are now changing our mindset to this: we, as delightful and fascinating women, are not looking for another man to date, another lover to make out with, nor another boyfriend to be with, but ***we are preparing ourselves to be found worthy of the king that God is bringing to us***.

Keeping 7 Keys for Life

Here are the seven keys, enticing peach, to keep your man happy and satisfied with you, once The Lord identifies, confirms, and brings *him* into your life:

Key number one: Respect

While the ideal woman craves to be loved, the ideal man needs to be respected. They want to know that their lives, their decisions, their capability of being a man and taking care of business is highly respected. You can show your man respect by allowing him to take the reins, made decisions, great or small, and choosing to follow his direction willingly and cheerfully. Compliment him on good choices he makes concerning himself or for you. Have a healthy submission to him in these matters and he will become a great leader over you.

Key number two: Appreciation

Men love it when their women appreciate anything they do for them. From grand to small or little to big, it makes him feel good about doing something for you when you show genuine thankfulness towards him. This builds his self esteem and causes his manhood to flourish, which becomes beneficial for you. Men then feel like they are doing something right when you appreciate it, which encourages more of that behavior, as well as a desire to be around you more.

Key number three: Honor

The best girls show their man the honor that makes him feel like he can fly over any obstacle. Treating him special due to his own uniqueness, empowers him to be a great man. It bolsters his self-esteem, self-confidence, and self-worth, and makes him feel like he can overcome and accomplish anything. It also causes him to favor those who show him honor. This is something that a wise man encouraged us to do: to seek the favor of man, along with the favor of God. The best way to receive this favor is to show honor to the person.

Key number four: Love

Men want to experience love that they cannot get from their parents, their male buddies, or a child. They want a woman who is not afraid to love them. This type of love is not afraid to reach out first, in full transparency. It risks sharing characteristics of love, such as kindness, tenderness, gentleness, and affection, hoping for a reciprocal response. Loving thoughts, behavior, and words that flow out of a woman at most or all times, is sure to be surrounded by those who want to experience her love.

Key number five: Softness

Just as a natural woman loves to see a man operate in his strength of masculinity, men also enjoy being with a woman in her softness of femininity. Perfecting the art of softness, which is a key concept of femininity, will melt the heart of a masculine man. Think, speak, act very soft, which all means that you need to be very girly through these methods: being gentle, moving slow, using a higher pitched voice, embodying sweetness, dressing in light, bright, feminine clothes, maturing in the sensuous arts, and acting with a lightheartedness.

Key number six: Excellence

In pursuing the high art of excellence, one must work on the aesthetic and the esoteric.

Keep yourself updated by caring for

your whole appearance. It's not fair to expect a man to set you above all women, when you know he is naturally attracted to pretty things, and you not give him something lovely to look at every day. It's one of the most important tasks you have sparkling cider!

Now be alluring, but not just by looking attractive, but by also being interesting to converse with. Seek to learn new things, keep current in events, and get involved in physical activities to stay fresh and knowledgeable. Extend your efforts you put into yourself to your living quarters. This way you are in harmony with yourself and your environment.

Key number seven: Kneeology

You will now need to create a custom of regularly getting on your knees to intercede for your relationship. Here are some things you should focus on in prayer.

Pray for:
*The things you experience, especially with your partner
*The vision God has for your relationship
*Your individual needs, growth, and protection
*The fruit of the Spirit to blossom within your spirit.

*That God will continuously teach you how to love your mate

Use these keys often, dear nutella dip, and your man will be happy and enjoy being around you...

Reflections – Questions & Activities

1. Which of the four women do you connect with the most?

Why?

2. What are five ways you can incorporate her song into your life?

a.

b.

c.

d.

e.

3. How do you plan to counter the opposition that might arise by following her example?

4. If there is a man in your life now, have you sought the Lord on what role he is to play in your life?

If yes, what is that role?

Have you accepted this and adjusted your response to him?

5. Is there something you can learn from each of the women we have

studied here?

a.

b.

c.

d.

6. How can you promote Biblical Womanhood and Femininity to other women, younger and older, in your circle?

7. Is it possible to start a group, whether online or at your church that centers on this topic, and uses this book as one of your guides to

conduct in relationships? Write down ideas, names, and places you can create a support group.

8. Would you be interested in sharing your story with my followers via social media? If so, please contact me.

Spiritual Insurance and Covenant

If you've been reading this material and currently are not connected to God, whose Name is the Lord, Almighty, "I Am that I Am", let's take this opportunity to rejoin ourselves with Him. He desires to communicate with you just like it was in the beginning of time. There may be many paths in life, but only one way to God, and that is through His Son, Jesus Christ, (Yashua ben Adonai, bey Ivrit) the Messiah of all nations.

To reconnect with Him is easy, yet powerful. The Bible says in Romans Chapter 10, verses 9 & 10, that if you confess with your mouth and believe in your Heart that God raised [Jesus] from the dead, you will be saved. Your heart's belief brings you to righteousness and your confession brings you salvation. Many have made Jesus their Savior, but not their Lord nor King. They believe in Him, but don't allow Him to be Lord and King over their lives by letting Him guide, teach, and direct them.

To be Saved, you must allow Him to be all three to you, according to Matthew 7:21-23.

If you declare this prayer out loud & sincerely believe it, you will truly come into His Kingdom and not a religion:

Oh Father,

Forgive my sin, for I was born into it. But I know you sent your only firstborn Son to come and die for me, in my place. He destroyed all the works of the enemy and gave me power to do so too. You raised Him from the dead, that I might have eternal life with You. I receive Him as my Savior, my Lord, and my King. Fill me with your Spirit and guide me in life to my purpose and destiny. Teach me to live for You and carry your nature. I love You and thank You for this opportunity to become one with you again.

In Jesus Name,

Amen

If you have prayed that in genuineness and out loud (both the natural and spiritual realms need to hear your decree, that's why when you are asked to make a vow or renounce something you must speak it audibly), then welcome to a Kingdom of righteousness, peace, and joy!! A Kingdom without end and with true abundance of love, pleasure, and life!

Write me at thefeminineprincess@gmail.com, if you prayed this, so I can send you a welcome gift for entering the family of Christ! Make sure you write in the subject field "Accepted Christ via your book (fill in the title)". Also, please notate if you are a Woman pursing femininity!

Start reading the Bible to learn His ways, surround yourself with similar minds, study related materials or media, and listen to praise / worship songs. Be cautious and ask the Spirit for discernment on what you watch, what you listen to, and who you hang around. The Lord will reveal truth, motives, and secrets to help your spiritual growth and the Holy Spirit will guide you away from any false way, if you are willing to follow Him.

About the Author

Olive Swan is a Feminine Expressive Arts Consultant and a Professional member of the International Expressive Arts Therapy Association. She shares the depth of femininity through various art modalities. Olive takes pleasure in all things girly, most things pastel, and some things Mediterranean. She wrote _33 Day Devotional for Feminine Women_, _39 Elements of Femininity_, _How to Get & Keep King_ and _50 Best Dance Quotes_ to help others blossom in the spirit and energy of a feminine woman. She also held conference calls on various feminine topics that are open to the general public.

She also wrote _7 Wealth Laws every believer should live by_ and _8 Timeless Lessons on Wealth_. Her artwork also reflects her spiritual interpretations and can be viewed and/or purchased at https://www.saatchiart.com/oliveswan.

Her quest to become ultra-feminine blossomed in 5775

(2014). Since then, she has studied feminine nature, women, girls, objects, books, colors, textiles, art, etc. Being more feminine has changed her approach to life, other people, as well as her decor. She believes being feminine is a high-class art that is available to all who wish it upon themselves.

Contact

Want to keep up to date with upcoming seminars, class, & workshops? Request to be added to our email list at connect@oliveswan.pink.

Want to work with a feminine consultant to explore more artistic ways to deepen and broaden your femininity? Request a session with me, a Feminine Expressive Art Consultant trained in the arts of femininity and the process of using the arts to grow at

www.oliveswan.pink.

Want a free e-book? Sign up at https://thefeminineprincess.com/free-e-book/ for my 18 Ways to Become Feminine Fast!

Also, you can learn more about femininity, order our feminine goods, participate in our services, or send a request, suggestion, or comment by:

main site:

www.oliveswan.pink

*blog site:

https://thefeminineprincess.com

*YouTube:

https://www.youtube.com/thefeminineprincess

*our store

https://oliveswan.pink/pink-peach-cream

*fiverr:

https://www.fiverr.com/oliveswan

classes on CD:

https://oliveswan.pink/pink-peach-cream

instagram:

http://instagram.com/thefeminineprincess

pinterest:

https://www.pinterest.com/thefeminineprincess

twitter:

https://twitter.com/feminineolive

*email:

thefeminineprincess@gmail.com

God Bless You and Your Feminine Journey! :-)

~Notes~

~Notes~

~Notes~

~Notes~

~Notes~

~Notes~

~Notes~

~Notes~

~Notes~

~Notes~

~Notes~

~Notes~

~Notes~

~Notes~

~Notes~

~Notes~

~Notes~

~Notes~

~Notes~

~Notes~

~Notes~

~Notes~

~Notes~

~Notes~

~Notes~

~Notes~

~Notes~

Made in the USA
Coppell, TX
20 July 2023